T5-CVJ-954

Year by Year

by F. Isabel Campoy

illustrated by Keri Lee Marino

Harcourt

Orlando Boston Dallas Chicago San Diego

Visit *The Learning Site!*

www.harcourtschool.com

This is me when I was one year old.

When I was one, I started to walk. Sometimes I fell down, but I didn't give up.

This is me when I was two years old.

When I was two, I started to talk. Sometimes I didn't make sense, but I didn't give up.

This is me when I was three years old.

When I was three, I started to make friends. Sometimes I cried, but I didn't give up.

This is me when I was four years old.

When I was four, I started to dress myself. Sometimes I put my shoes on the wrong feet, but I didn't give up.

This is me when I was five years old.

When I was five, I started to ride a bike. Sometimes I fell off, but I didn't give up.

This is me when I was six
years old.

When I was six, I started to read. Sometimes I made mistakes, but I didn't give up.

This is me now. I am seven years old.

My family moved to the United States. I am learning English. Sometimes I don't understand the words, but I won't give up.

Next year, I will be eight years old. What will I start to do when I am eight? I can't wait!